The Key Facts™ on

Syria

Essential Information on Syria

By Patrick W. Nee

The Internationalist®

www.internationalist.com

Syria is in the midst of a civil conflict. This may or may not affect the core information on this country

The Internationalist®

International Business, Investment, and Travel

Published by:

The Internationalist Publishing Company

96 Walter Street/ Suite 200

Boston, MA 02131, USA

Tel: 617-354-7722

www.internationalist.com

PN@internationalist.com

Table Of Contents

Chapter 1: Background

Following World War I, France acquired a mandate over the northern portion of the former Ottoman Empire province of Syria. The French administered the area as Syria until granting it independence in 1946. The new country lacked political stability, however, and experienced a series of military coups during its first decades. Syria united with Egypt in February 1958 to form the United Arab Republic. In September 1961, the two entities separated, and the Syrian Arab Republic was reestablished. In November 1970, Hafiz al-ASAD, a member of the socialist Ba'th Party and the minority Alawi sect, seized power in a bloodless coup and brought political stability to the country. In the 1967 Arab-Israeli War, Syria lost the Golan Heights to Israel. During the 1990s, Syria and Israel held occasional peace talks over its return. Following the death of President al-ASAD, his son, Bashar al-ASAD, was approved as president by popular referendum in July 2000. Syrian troops - stationed in Lebanon since 1976 in an ostensible peacekeeping role - were withdrawn in April 2005. During the July-August 2006 conflict between Israel and Hizballah, Syria placed its military forces on alert but did not intervene directly on behalf of its ally Hizballah. In May 2007 Bashar al-ASAD's second term as president was approved by popular referendum. Influenced by major uprisings that began elsewhere in the region, antigovernment protests broke out in the southern province of Dar'a in March 2011 with protesters calling for the repeal of the restrictive Emergency Law allowing arrests without charge, the legalization of political parties, and the removal of corrupt local officials. Since then demonstrations and unrest have spread to nearly every city in Syria, but the size and intensity of protests have fluctuated over time. The government responded to unrest with a mix of concessions - including the repeal of the Emergency Law and approving new laws permitting new political parties and liberalizing local and national elections - and force. However, the government's response has failed to meet opposition demands for ASAD to step down, and the government's ongoing security operations to quell unrest and widespread armed opposition activity have led to extended violent clashes between government forces and oppositionists. International pressure on the ASAD regime has intensified since late 2011 as the Arab League, EU, Turkey, and the United States have expanded economic sanctions against the regime. Lakhdar BRAHIMI, current Joint Special Representative of the United Nations and the League of Arab States on the Syrian crisis, in October 2012 began meeting with regional heads of state to assist in brokering a cease-fire. In December 2012, the National Coalition of Syrian Revolution and Opposition Forces was recognized by more than 130 countries as the sole legitimate representative of the Syrian people. Unrest persists in 2013,and the death toll among Syrian government forces, Opposition Forces, and civilians has topped 60,000.

Chapter 2: Geography

Location:

    Middle East, bordering the Mediterranean Sea, between Lebanon and Turkey

Geographic coordinates:

    35 00 N, 38 00 E

Map references:

    Middle East

Area:

    <u>total</u>: 185,180 sq km

    <u>country comparison to the world</u>: 89

    <u>land</u>: 183,630 sq km

    <u>water</u>: 1,550 sq km

    <u>note</u>: includes 1,295 sq km of Israeli-occupied territory

Area - comparative:

    slightly larger than North Dakota

Land boundaries:

    <u>total</u>: 2,253 km

    <u>border countries</u>: Iraq 605 km, Israel 76 km, Jordan 375 km, Lebanon 375 km, Turkey 822 km

Coastline:

    193 km

Maritime claims:

    <u>territorial sea</u>: 12 nm

    <u>contiguous zone</u>: 24 nm

Climate:

    mostly desert; hot, dry, sunny summers (June to August) and mild, rainy winters (December to February) along coast; cold weather with snow or sleet periodically in Damascus

Terrain:

    primarily semiarid and desert plateau; narrow coastal plain; mountains in west

Elevation extremes:

    <u>lowest point</u>: unnamed location near Lake Tiberias -200 m

    <u>highest point</u>: Mount Hermon 2,814 m

Natural resources:

petroleum, phosphates, chrome and manganese ores, asphalt, iron ore, rock salt, marble, gypsum, hydropower

Land use:

arable land: 24.8%

permanent crops: 4.47%

other: 70.73% (2005)

Irrigated land:

13,560 sq km (2003)

Total renewable water resources:

46.1 cu km (1997)

Freshwater withdrawal (domestic/industrial/agricultural):

total: 19.95 cu km/yr (3%/2%/95%)

per capita: 1,048 cu m/yr (2000)

Natural hazards:

dust storms, sandstorms

volcanism: Syria's two historically active volcanoes, Es Safa and an unnamed volcano near the Turkish border have not erupted in centuries

Environment - current issues:

deforestation; overgrazing; soil erosion; desertification; water pollution from raw sewage and petroleum refining wastes; inadequate potable water

Environment - international agreements:

party to: Biodiversity, Climate Change, Climate Change-Kyoto Protocol, Desertification, Endangered Species, Hazardous Wastes, Ozone Layer Protection, Ship Pollution, Wetlands

signed, but not ratified: Environmental Modification

Geography - note:

the capital of Damascus - located at an oasis fed by the Barada River - is thought to be one of the world's oldest continuously inhabited cities; there are 41 Israeli settlements and civilian land use sites in the Israeli-occupied Golan Heights (2010 est.)

Chapter 3: People and Society

Nationality:

noun: Syrian(s)

adjective: Syrian

Ethnic groups:

Arab 90.3%, Kurds, Armenians, and other 9.7%

Languages:

Arabic (official), Kurdish, Armenian, Aramaic, Circassian (widely understood); French, English (somewhat understood)

Religions:

Sunni Muslim (Islam - official) 74%, other Muslim (includes Alawite, Druze) 16%, Christian (various denominations) 10%, Jewish (tiny communities in Damascus, Al Qamishli, and Aleppo)

Population:

22,457,336 (July 2013 est.)

country comparison to the world: 53

note: approximately 18,700 Israeli settlers live in the Golan Heights (2011)

Age structure:

0-14 years: 34.6% (male 3,990,769/female 3,793,859)

15-24 years: 21.1% (male 2,431,142/female 2,326,152)

25-54 years: 36.1% (male 4,140,624/female 4,001,430)

55-64 years: 4.4% (male 487,540/female 501,217)

65 years and over: 3.8% (male 393,984/female 464,029) (2012 est.)

Median age:

total: 22.3 years

male: 22.1 years

female: 22.5 years (2012 est.)

Population growth rate:

-0.797% (2012 est.)

country comparison to the world: 226

Birth rate:

23.52 births/1,000 population (2012 est.)

country comparison to the world: 71

Death rate:

3.67 deaths/1,000 population (July 2012 est.)

country comparison to the world: 210

Net migration rate:

-27.82 migrant(s)/1,000 population (2012 est.)

country comparison to the world: 219

Urbanization:

urban population: 56% of total population (2010)

rate of urbanization: 2.5% annual rate of change (2010-15 est.)

Major cities - population:

Aleppo 2.985 million; DAMASCUS (capital) 2.527 million; Hims 1.276 million; Hamah 854,000 (2009)

Sex ratio:

at birth: 1.06 male(s)/female

under 15 years: 1.05 male(s)/female

15-64 years: 1.03 male(s)/female

65 years and over: 0.85 male(s)/female

total population: 1.03 male(s)/female (2011 est.)

Maternal mortality rate:

70 deaths/100,000 live births (2010)

country comparison to the world: 88

Infant mortality rate:

total: 15.12 deaths/1,000 live births

country comparison to the world: 114

male: 17.38 deaths/1,000 live births

female: 12.72 deaths/1,000 live births (2012 est.)

Life expectancy at birth:

total population: 74.92 years

country comparison to the world: 95

male: 72.53 years

female: 77.45 years (2012 est.)

Total fertility rate:

2.77 children born/woman (2013 est.)

Health expenditures:

3.4% of GDP (2010)

country comparison to the world: 178

Physicians density:

1.5 physicians/1,000 population (2008)

Hospital bed density:

1.5 beds/1,000 population (2010)

Sanitation facility access:

improved:

urban: 96% of population

rural: 95% of population

total: 96% of population

unimproved:

urban: 4% of population

rural: 5% of population

total: 4% of population

HIV/AIDS - adult prevalence rate:

less than 0.1% (2001 est.)

country comparison to the world: 157

HIV/AIDS - people living with HIV/AIDS:

fewer than 500 (2003 est.)

country comparison to the world: 153

HIV/AIDS - deaths:

fewer than 200 (2003 est.)

country comparison to the world: 114

Children under the age of 5 years underweight:

10% (2006)

country comparison to the world: 66

Education expenditures:

4.9% of GDP (2007)

country comparison to the world: 60

Literacy:

definition: age 15 and over can read and write

total population: 79.6%

male: 86%

female: 73.6% (2004 census)

School life expectancy (primary to tertiary education):

total: 11 years

male: 12 years

female: 11 years (2007)

Unemployment, youth ages 15-24:

total: 19.2%

country comparison to the world: 63

male: 15.3%

female: 40.2% (2010)

Chapter 4: Government and Key Leaders

Government Note:

Syria is in the midst of a civil conflict. This may or may not affect the core information on the country's government and leaders.

Country name:

conventional long form: Syrian Arab Republic

conventional short form: Syria

local long form: Al Jumhuriyah al Arabiyah as Suriyah

local short form: Suriyah

former: United Arab Republic (with Egypt)

Government type:

republic under an authoritarian regime

Capital:

name: Damascus

geographic coordinates: 33 30 N, 36 18 E

time difference: UTC+2 (7 hours ahead of Washington, DC during Standard Time)

daylight saving time: +1hr, begins midnight on the last Friday in March; ends at midnight on the last Friday in October

Administrative divisions:

14 provinces (muhafazat, singular - muhafazah); Al Hasakah, Al Ladhiqiyah (Latakia), Al Qunaytirah, Ar Raqqah, As Suwayda', Dar'a, Dayr az Zawr, Dimashq (Damascus), Halab, Hamah, Hims (Homs), Idlib, Rif Dimashq (Damascus Countryside), Tartus

Independence:

17 April 1946 (from League of Nations mandate under French administration)

National holiday:

Independence Day, 17 April (1946)

Constitution:

13 March 1973; amended February 2012

Legal system:

mixed legal system of civil and Islamic law (for family courts)

International law organization participation:

has not submitted an ICJ jurisdiction declaration; non-party state to the ICCt

Suffrage:

18 years of age; universal

Executive branch:

chief of state: President Bashar al-ASAD (since 17 July 2000); Vice President Farouk al-SHARA (since 21 February 2006) oversees foreign policy; Vice President Najah al-ATTAR (since 23 March 2006) oversees cultural policy

head of government: Prime Minister Wael al-HALQI (since 9 August 2012)

cabinet: Council of Ministers appointed by the president; note - new Council appointed on 14 April 2011

elections: president approved by popular referendum for a second seven-year term (no term limits); referendum last held on 27 May 2007 (next to be held in May 2014); the president appoints the vice presidents, prime minister, and deputy prime ministers

election results: Bashar al-ASAD approved as president; percent of vote - Bashar al-ASAD 97.6%, other 2.4%

Legislative branch:

unicameral People's Assembly or Majlis al-Shaab (250 seats; members elected by popular vote to serve four-year terms)

elections: last held on 7 May 2012 (next to be held in 2016)

election results: percent of vote by party - NA; seats by party - NA

Judicial branch:

Supreme Judicial Council (appoints and dismisses judges; headed by the president); national level - Supreme Constitutional Court (adjudicates electoral disputes and rules on constitutionality of laws and decrees; justices appointed for four-year terms by the president); Court of Cassation; Appeals Courts (Appeals Courts represent an intermediate level between the Court of Cassation and local level courts); local level - Magistrate Courts; Courts of First Instance; Juvenile Courts; Customs Courts; specialized courts - Economic Security Courts (hear cases related to economic crimes); Supreme State Security Court (hear cases related to national security); Personal Status Courts (religious; hear cases related to marriage and divorce)

Political parties and leaders:

legal parties: National Progressive Front or NPF [President Bashar al-ASAD, Dr. Suleiman QADDAH] (includes Arab Socialist Renaissance (Ba'th) Party [President Bashar al-ASAD]; Socialist Unionist Democratic Party [Fadlallah Nasr Al-DIN]; Syrian Arab Socialist Union or ASU [Safwan al-QUDSI]; Syrian Communist Party (two branches) [Wissal Farha BAKDASH,

Yusuf Rashid FAYSAL]; Syrian Social Nationalist Party [As'ad HARDAN]; Unionist Socialist Party [Fayez ISMAIL])

Kurdish parties (considered illegal): Kurdish Azadi Party; Kurdish Democratic Accord Party (al Wifaq); Kurdish Democratic Party (al Parti-Ibrahim wing); Kurdish Democratic Party (al Parti-Mustafa wing); Kurdish Democratic Party in Syria or KDP-S; Kurdish Democratic Patriotic/National Party; Kurdish Democratic Progressive Party or KDPP-Darwish; Kurdish Democratic Progressive Party or KDPP-Muhammad; Kurdish Democratic Union Party or PYD [Salih Muslim MOHAMMAD]; Kurdish Democratic Unity Party; Kurdish Democratic Yekiti Party; Kurdish Future Party or KFP; Kurdish Future Party [Rezan HASSAN]; Kurdish Left Party; Kurdish Yekiti (Union) Party; Syrian Kurdish Democratic Party

other parties: Syrian Democratic Party [Mustafa QALAAJI]

Political pressure groups and leaders:

Free Syrian Army; National Coalition of Syrian Revolution and Oppositon Forces or Syrian Oppositon Coalition [Mu'aaz al-KHATIB] (operates in exile in Cairo); Syrian Muslim Brotherhood or SMB [Muhammad Riyad al-SHAQFAH] (operates in exile in London)

note - there are also hundreds of local groups that organize protests and stage armed attacks

International organization participation:

ABEDA, AFESD, AMF, CAEU, FAO, G-24, G-77, IAEA, IBRD, ICAO, ICC (national committees), ICRM, IDA, IDB, IFAD, IFC, IFRCS, IHO, ILO, IMF, IMO, Interpol, IOC, IPU, ISO, ITSO, ITU, MIGA, NAM, OAPEC, OIC, UN, UNCTAD, UNESCO, UNIDO, UNRWA, UNWTO, UPU, WCO, WFTU (NGOs), WHO, WIPO, WMO, WTO (observer)

Diplomatic representation in the US:

chief of mission: Ambassador (vacant)

chancery: 2215 Wyoming Avenue NW, Washington, DC 20008

telephone: [1] (202) 232-6313

FAX: [1] (202) 265-4585

Diplomatic representation from the US:

chief of mission: Ambassador Robert S. FORD; note - on 6 February 2012, the US closed its embassy in Damascus

embassy: Abou Roumaneh, Al-Mansour Street, No. 2, Damascus

mailing address: P. O. Box 29, Damascus

telephone: [963] (11) 3391-4444

FAX: [963] (11) 3391-3999

Key Leaders

Pres.	Bashar al-ASAD
Vice Pres.	Farouk al-SHARA
Vice Pres.	Najah al-ATTAR
Prime Min.	Wael al-HALQI
Dep. Prime Min.	Fahd Jasim al-FURAYJ, *Lt. Gen.*
Dep. Prime Min.	Walid al-MUALEM
Dep. Prime Min. for Economic Affairs	Qadri JAMIL
Dep. Prime Min. for Services Affairs	Umar Ibrahim GHALAWANJI
Min. of Agriculture	Ahmad al-QADRI
Min. of Culture	Lubanah MUSHAWEH
Min. of Defense	Fahd Jasim al-FURAYJ, *Lt. Gen.*
Min. of Domestic Trade & Consumer Protection	Samir Izzat Qadi AMIN
Min. of Economy & Foreign Trade	Khodr URFALI
Min. of Education	Hazwan al-WAZZ
Min. of Electricity	Imad Muhammad Deeb KHAMIS
Min. of Finance	Ismael ISMAEL
Min. of Foreign & Expatriate Affairs	Walid al-MUALEM
Min. of Health	Sa'd Abd al-Salam NAYIF
Min. of Higher Education	Malik ALI
Min. of Housing & Urban Development	Hussein FARZAT
Min. of Industry	Kamal al-Din TUMAH
Min. of Information	Umran Ahid al-ZA'BI
Min. of the Interior	Muhammad Ibrahim al-SHA'AR
Min. of Justice	Najim Hamad al-AHMAD
Min. of Labor	Hassan HIJAZI
Min. of Local Admin.	Umar Ibrahim GHALAWANJI
Min. of Petroleum & Mineral Wealth	Suleiman al-ABBAS
Min. of Presidential Affairs	Mansur Fadlallah AZZAM
Min. of Public Works	Yasser al-SIBA'I
Min. of Religious Endowments	Muhammad Abd al-Sattar al-SAYYID
Min. of Social Affairs	Jasim Muhammad ZAKARIYA
Min. of Telecommunication & Technology	Imad SABBUNI
Min. of Tourism	Bashar Riyad YAZIGI
Min. of Transport	Mahmoud Ibrahim SAID
Min. of Water Resources	Bassam HANNA
Min. of State	Husayn Mahmud FARZAT

Min. of State	Abdallah Khalil HUSAYN
Min. of State	Najm al-Din KHRIIT
Min. of State	Muhammad Turki al-SAYYID
Min. of State	Jamal Shaaban SHAHEEN
Min. of State	Hasib Elias SHAMMAS
Min. of State	Joseph SUWAYD
Min. of State for Environmental Affairs	Nazira Farah SARKIS
Min. of State for National Reconciliation Affairs	Ali HAYDAR
Governor, Central Bank	Adib MAYALA
Ambassador to the US	
Permanent Representative to the UN, New York	Bashar al-JAFARI

Flag description:

three equal horizontal bands of red (top), white, and black; two small, green, five-pointed stars in a horizontal line centered in the white band; the band colors derive from the Arab Liberation flag and represent oppression (black), overcome through bloody struggle (red), to be replaced by a bright future (white); identical to the former flag of the United Arab Republic (1958-1961) where the two stars represented the constituent states of Syria and Egypt; the current design dates to 1980

note: similar to the flag of Yemen, which has a plain white band, Iraq, which has an Arabic inscription centered in the white band, and that of Egypt, which has a gold Eagle of Saladin centered in the white band

National symbol(s):

hawk

National anthem:

name: "Humat ad-Diyar" (Guardians of the Homeland)

lyrics/music: Khalil Mardam BEY/Mohammad Salim FLAYFEL and Ahmad Salim FLAYFEL

note: adopted 1936, restored 1961; between 1958 and 1961, while Syria was a member of the United Arab Republic with Egypt, the country had a different anthem

Chapter 5: Economy

Economy - overview:

Despite modest economic growth and reform prior to the outbreak of unrest, Syria's economy continues to suffer the effects of the ongoing conflict that began in 2011. The economy further contracted in 2012 because of international sanctions and reduced domestic consumption and production. The government has struggled to address the effects of economic decline, including dwindling foreign exchange reserves, rising budget and trade deficits, and the decreasing value of the Syrian pound. Prior to the unrest, Damascus began liberalizing economic policies, including cutting lending interest rates, opening private banks, consolidating multiple exchange rates, raising prices on some subsidized items, and establishing the Damascus Stock Exchange. The economy remains highly regulated by the government. Long-run economic constraints include foreign trade barriers, declining oil production, high unemployment, rising budget deficits, and increasing pressure on water supplies caused by heavy use in agriculture, rapid population growth, industrial expansion, and water pollution.

GDP (purchasing power parity):

$107.6 billion (2011 est.)

country comparison to the world: 69

$110.1 billion (2010 est.)

$106.5 billion (2009 est.)

note: data are in 2012 US dollars

GDP (official exchange rate):

$64.7 billion (2011 est.)

GDP - real growth rate:

NA (2012 est.)

-2.3% (2011 est.)

3.4% (2010 est.)

GDP - per capita (PPP):

$5,100 (2011 est.)

country comparison to the world: 153

$5,100 (2010 est.)

$5,200 (2009 est.)

note: data are in 2011 US dollars

GDP - composition by sector:

agriculture: 18.1%

industry: 25.3%

services: 56.6% (2012 est.)

Labor force:

5.54 million (2012 est.)

country comparison to the world: 71

Labor force - by occupation:

agriculture: 17%

industry: 16%

services: 67% (2008 est.)

Unemployment rate:

18% (2012 est.)

country comparison to the world: 155

14.9% (2011 est.)

Population below poverty line:

11.9% (2006 est.)

Investment (gross fixed):

20.8% of GDP (2012 est.)

country comparison to the world: 86

Budget:

revenues: $6.511 billion

expenditures: $12.68 billion (2012 est.)

Taxes and other revenues:

10.1% of GDP (2012 est.)

country comparison to the world: 207

Budget surplus (+) or deficit (-):

-9.5% of GDP (2012 est.)

country comparison to the world: 199

Public debt:

44% of GDP (2012 est.)

country comparison to the world: 77

35.2% of GDP (2011 est.)

Inflation rate (consumer prices):

33.7% (2012 est.)

country comparison to the world: 222

4.8% (2011 est.)

Central bank discount rate:

0.75% (31 December 2012 est.)

country comparison to the world: 73

5% (31 December 2011 est.)

Commercial bank prime lending rate:

11.7% (31 December 2012 est.)

country comparison to the world: 86

10.5% (31 December 2011 est.)

Stock of narrow money:

$18.01 billion (31 December 2012 est.)

country comparison to the world: 65

$22.37 billion (31 December 2011 est.)

Stock of broad money:

$30.17 billion (31 December 2012 est.)

country comparison to the world: 76

$39.36 billion (31 December 2011 est.)

Stock of domestic credit:

$20.33 billion (31 December 2012 est.)

country comparison to the world: 82

$27.8 billion (31 December 2011 est.)

Agriculture - products:

wheat, barley, cotton, lentils, chickpeas, olives, sugar beets; beef, mutton, eggs, poultry, milk

Industries:

petroleum, textiles, food processing, beverages, tobacco, phosphate rock mining, cement, oil seeds crushing, car assembly

Industrial production growth rate:

6% (2010 est.)

country comparison to the world: 53

Current account balance:

-$5.103 billion (2012 est.)

country comparison to the world: 167
-$7.726 billion (2011 est.)

Exports:

$4.981 billion (2012 est.)

country comparison to the world: 114

$10.29 billion (2011 est.)

Exports - commodities:

crude oil, minerals, petroleum products, fruits and vegetables, cotton fiber, textiles, clothing, meat and live animals, wheat

Exports - partners:

Iraq 38.8%, Italy 7.9%, Germany 7.1%, Saudi Arabia 6.5%, Kuwait 4.2% (2011)

Imports:

$10.01 billion (2012 est.)

country comparison to the world: 97

$17.6 billion (2011 est.)

Imports - commodities:

machinery and transport equipment, electric power machinery, food and livestock, metal and metal products, chemicals and chemical products, plastics, yarn, paper

Imports - partners:

Saudi Arabia 14.8%, China 10.3%, UAE 7.3%, Turkey 6.8%, Iran 5.4%, Italy 5.1%, Russia 4.6%, Iraq 4.4% (2011)

Reserves of foreign exchange and gold:

$4.774 billion (31 December 2012 est.)

country comparison to the world: 93

$14.83 billion (31 December 2011 est.)

Debt - external:

$8.818 billion (31 December 2012 est.)

country comparison to the world: 99

$8.196 billion (31 December 2011 est.)

Exchange rates:

Syrian pounds (SYP) per US dollar -
63.94 (2012 est.)
48.371 (2011 est.)
11.225 (2010 est.)

46.708 (2009)

46.5281 (2008)

Fiscal year:

calendar year

Chapter 6: Energy

Electricity - production:

    40.86 billion kWh (2009 est.)

    country comparison to the world: 58

Electricity - consumption:

    28.87 billion kWh (2009 est.)

    country comparison to the world: 63

Electricity - exports:

    0 kWh (2010 est.)

    country comparison to the world: 134

Electricity - imports:

    0 kWh (2010 est.)

    country comparison to the world: 137

Electricity - installed generating capacity:

    8.2 million kW (2009 est.)

    country comparison to the world: 62

Electricity - from fossil fuels:

    84.8% of total installed capacity (2009 est.)

    country comparison to the world: 86

Electricity - from nuclear fuels:

    0% of total installed capacity (2009 est.)

    country comparison to the world: 181

Electricity - from hydroelectric plants:

    15.2% of total installed capacity (2009 est.)

    country comparison to the world: 104

Electricity - from other renewable sources:

    0% of total installed capacity (2009 est.)

    country comparison to the world: 189

Crude oil - production:

    333,900 bbl/day (2011 est.)

    country comparison to the world: 33

Crude oil - exports:

144,000 bbl/day (2009 est.)

country comparison to the world: 34

Crude oil - imports:

0 bbl/day (2009 est.)

country comparison to the world: 124

Crude oil - proved reserves:

2.183 billion bbl (1 January 2012 est.)

country comparison to the world: 35

Refined petroleum products - production:

255,600 bbl/day (2008 est.)

country comparison to the world: 49

Refined petroleum products - consumption:

258,800 bbl/day (2011 est.)

country comparison to the world: 50

Refined petroleum products - exports:

14,540 bbl/day (2008 est.)

country comparison to the world: 83

Refined petroleum products - imports:

58,160 bbl/day (2008 est.)

country comparison to the world: 66

Natural gas - production:

8.94 billion cu m (2010 est.)

country comparison to the world: 45

Natural gas - consumption:

9.63 billion cu m (2010 est.)

country comparison to the world: 48

Natural gas - exports:

0 cu m (2010 est.)

country comparison to the world: 58

Natural gas - imports:

690 million cu m (2010 est.)

country comparison to the world: 66

Natural gas - proved reserves:

240.7 billion cu m (1 January 2012 est.)

<u>country comparison to the world</u>: 45

Carbon dioxide emissions from consumption of energy:

63.1 million Mt (2010 est.)

<u>country comparison to the world</u>: 54

Chapter 7: Communications

Telephones - main lines in use:

4.345 million (2011)

country comparison to the world: 37

Telephones - mobile cellular:

13.117 million (2011)

country comparison to the world: 59

Telephone system:

general assessment: fair system currently undergoing significant improvement and digital upgrades, including fiber-optic technology and expansion of the network to rural areas; the armed insurgency that began in 2011 has led to major disruptions to the network and has caused telephone and Internet outages throughout the country

domestic: the number of fixed-line connections has increased markedly since 2000; mobile-cellular service growing with telephone subscribership nearly 60 per 100 persons in 2011

international: country code - 963; submarine cable connection to Egypt, Lebanon, and Cyprus; satellite earth stations - 1 Intelsat (Indian Ocean) and 1 Intersputnik (Atlantic Ocean region); coaxial cable and microwave radio relay to Iraq, Jordan, Lebanon, and Turkey; participant in Medarabtel

Broadcast media:

state-run TV and radio broadcast networks; state operates 2 TV networks and a satellite channel; roughly two-thirds of Syrian homes have a satellite dish providing access to foreign TV broadcasts; 3 state-run radio channels; first private radio station launched in 2005; private radio broadcasters prohibited from transmitting news or political content (2007)

Internet country code:

.sy

Internet hosts:

416 (2012)

country comparison to the world: 188

Internet users:

4.469 million (2009)

country comparison to the world: 52

Chapter 8: Transportation

Airports:

> 99 (2012)
>
> country comparison to the world: 58

Airports - with paved runways:

> total: 29
>
> over 3,047 m: 5
>
> 2,438 to 3,047 m: 16
>
> 914 to 1,523 m: 3
>
> under 914 m: 5 (2012)

Airports - with unpaved runways:

> total: 70
>
> 1,524 to 2,437 m: 1
>
> 914 to 1,523 m: 14
>
> under 914 m: 55 (2012)

Heliports:

> 6 (2012)

Pipelines:

> gas 3,161 km; oil 1,997 km (2010)

Railways:

> total: 2,052 km
>
> country comparison to the world: 72
>
> standard gauge: 1,801 km 1.435-m gauge
>
> narrow gauge: 251 km 1.050-m gauge (2008)

Roadways:

> total: 68,157 km
>
> country comparison to the world: 67
>
> paved: 61,514 km (includes 1,103 km of expressways)
>
> unpaved: 6,643 km (2006)

Waterways:

> 900 km (navigable but not economically significant) (2011)

country comparison to the world: 69

Merchant marine:

total: 19

country comparison to the world: 95

by type: bulk carrier 4, cargo 14, carrier 1

registered in other countries: 166 (Barbados 1, Belize 4, Bolivia 4, Cambodia 22, Comoros 5, Dominica 4, Georgia 24, Lebanon 2, Liberia 1, Malta 4, Moldova 5, North Korea 4, Panama 34, Saint Vincent and the Grenadines 9, Sierra Leone 13, Tanzania 23, Togo 6, unknown 1) (2010)

Ports and terminals:

Baniyas, Latakia, Tartus

Chapter 9: Military

Military branches:

Syrian Armed Forces: Syrian Arab Army, Syrian Arab Navy, Syrian Arab Air and Air Defense Forces (includes Air Defense Command) (2008)

Military service age and obligation:

18 years of age for compulsory male military service; conscript service obligation - 18 months; women are not conscripted but may volunteer to serve; re-enlistment obligation 5 years, with retirement after 15 years or age 40 (enlisted) or 20 years or age 45 (NCOs) (2010)

Manpower available for military service:

males age 16-49: 5,889,837

females age 16-49: 5,660,751 (2010 est.)

Manpower fit for military service:

males age 16-49: 5,055,510

females age 16-49: 4,884,151 (2010 est.)

Manpower reaching militarily significant age annually:

male: 256,698

female: 244,712 (2010 est.)

Military expenditures:

5.9% of GDP (2005 est.)

country comparison to the world: 10

Chapter 10: Transnational Issues

Disputes - international:

Golan Heights is Israeli-occupied with the almost 1,000-strong UN Disengagement Observer Force patrolling a buffer zone since 1964; lacking a treaty or other documentation describing the boundary, portions of the Lebanon-Syria boundary are unclear with several sections in dispute; since 2000, Lebanon has claimed Shab'a Farms in the Golan Heights; 2004 Agreement and pending demarcation settles border dispute with Jordan

Refugees and internally displaced persons:

refugees (country of origin): 101,244 (Iraq); 486,946 (Palestinian Refugees (UNRWA))

IDPs: more than 2 million (2011-2012 civil war) (2012)

Trafficking in persons:

current situation: Syria is principally a destination country for women and children subjected to forced labor or sex trafficking; women from Indonesia, the Philippines, Somalia, and Ethiopia are recruited by employment agencies to work in Syria as domestic servants, but are subsequently subjected to conditions of forced labor; some economically desperate Syrian children are subjected to conditions of forced labor within the country, particularly by organized street begging rings; some Syrian women in Lebanon may be forced to engage in street prostitution and small numbers of Syrian girls are reportedly brought to Lebanon for the purpose of prostitution

tier rating: Tier 2 Watch List - the government made modest anti-trafficking efforts, however, it did not demonstrate evidence of increasing efforts to investigate and punish trafficking offenses, inform the public about the practice of human trafficking, or provide much-needed anti-trafficking training to law enforcement and social welfare officials (2008)

Illicit drugs:

a transit point for opiates, hashish, and cocaine bound for regional and Western markets; weak anti-money-laundering controls and bank privatization may leave it vulnerable to money laundering

Other Key Facts™ Titles

Key Facts on Syria

Key Facts on China

Key Facts on Qatar

Key Facts on India

Key Facts on Germany

Key Facts on Argentina

Key Facts on Russia

Key Facts on North Korea

Key Facts on Brazil

Key Facts on Italy

Key Facts on the United Arab Emirates

Key Facts on the European Union

Key Facts on Pakistan

Key Facts on Saudi Arabia

Key Facts on Cyprus

Key Facts on Iran

Key Facts on Afghanistan

Key Facts on Iraq

Key Facts on Indonesia

Key Facts on South Korea

All Key Facts™ Titles are Available at www.Amazon.com

THE INTERNATIONALIST®

2013

www.internationalist.com

www.ingramcontent.com/pod-product-compliance
Lightning Source LLC
Chambersburg PA
CBHW072030190526
45166CB00015B/1732